Give Your Dog a Bone Series

TEACH YOUR DOG TO PEE AND POOP OUTSIDE

HOUSETRAINING MADE EASY

JennaLee Gallicchio

.   .   .   .   .

Published by
From Puppy To Pal Productions
Bedminster, NJ
FromPuppyToPal.com

.   .   .   .   .

Print Layout by
N.D. Author Services [NDAS]
www.NDAuthorServices.com

ALSO BY JENNALEE GALLICCHIO

*The Secret To Getting Your Dog To
Do What You Want*

*How to Turn Your Problem Pup into
Your Dream Dog*

DEDICATION

This book is dedicated to all the dogs who have chosen to live out their lives with me. I am constantly amazed and humbled by their joy of life and their unconditional love. Thank you for being so forgiving with me and all of the mistakes that I have made and am sure I will make in the future. I am grateful to have had and have such generous, gentle teachers!

Sydney   Mattie   Ryder   Emmy

THANKS

I want to thank all the dogs who have so graciously allowed me to work with and learn from them. And, most importantly, to their owners who do me the greatest honor by hiring me. It has been my extreme pleasure and greatest joy to work with all of you.

Thank you, thank you, thank you to all of you wonderful readers who have taken the time to buy and read this book! It means more than you will ever know.

Contents

CHAPTER 1:
TEACH YOUR DOG TO PEE AND POOP OUTSIDE

HOUSETRAINING MADE EASY

"It does not matter how slowly you go as long as you don't stop."
—Confucius

If I could name the top 3 behaviors that an owner would want to teach their dog, housetraining would be among them. It is one of the many reasons that dogs end up being given away or surrendered to a shelter. Sadly, it is also one of the easiest to fix.

I think that it is safe to assume that if you are reading this book it is because of two reasons:

- You have a new puppy or a new older dog and want to make sure that you get the housetraining right.

or

- You are at your wits end with a puppy or dog (s) who is peeing and pooping all over the house and you don't know how to make it stop.

I can safely say that you have come to the right place! If you choose to follow this book exactly, you too can have a pee and poop free home.

Although, for some, housetraining seems like an overwhelming, difficult task, it can actually be learned by your dog in just 30 days. Many clients (myself included) have even accomplished house-training in as little as 10 to 14 days.

Ryder, my puppy, was housetrained in 2 weeks. Granted, I was overly obsessive about the process and didn't expect him to hold it for longer than 7 hours overnight as he was 12 weeks old—even less when he was awake, but he started "telling" me that he had to go potty in a very clear way in as little as 14 days.

Had I not been watching him like a hawk, I would've missed him "telling" me that he had to go out.

Since I know how frustrating housetraining can seem, I have made sure to outline a simple process that will give you clear instructions.

I will teach you exactly what to do so that you can set your dog up for success and make having a housetrained pup a reality.

You will learn:

- What exactly housetraining is.

- The very first thing you should do if you are working with a dog who has been peeing and pooping in the house.

- Why dogs choose to pee and poop in certain places.

- How to set your dog up to be successful.

- Why it's easier to teach our dogs what we want them to do, rather than what not to do.

- How to let your pup EARN their right to roam free in your home.

- The tools that will help you to be successful.

- How to apply a housetraining routine.

- Putting the "duty" on a cue and teaching your pup to ring a bell.

- Understanding what your dogs "Tell" is, so that you can recognize when they are letting you know they have to go out.

Housetraining is an easy, but time consuming, process which is why so many people struggle with it. People also struggle and fail because they think their dog is housetrained before they actually are. When we make this mistake, we give our pup access to the entire house too soon and set them up to fail.

At the same time we make the housetraining process more difficult for ourselves.

By gradually allowing our dog to earn the right to have more and more exposure to our homes, we help set our dog up to fully understand where their bathroom is. And, honestly, housetraining is really setting our dog up for success by giving them multiple opportunities to pee and poop in the RIGHT place. Outside!

Keep in mind that, although you might be able to housetrain your dog in 10 to 14 days, the age of your dog will make a difference as to how long they can actually HOLD it.

For example, a puppy won't be able to hold their pee for an extended period (like 8 plus hours) until they are between 4 to 6 months of age because their bladder muscles aren't fully developed, whereas a dog over 6 months will be able to hold it easily because their bladder muscles are fully developed. (This is also why housetraining a puppy is an easier task than housetraining an older dog.)

So, although your dog may be giving you signals and letting you know they have to go out, they may not yet be able to hold it for extended periods of time. This doesn't mean they aren't housetrained, only that their bodies aren't fully developed.

Make sure that when you start housetraining you are dedicated to the process. Have patience with yourself and your pup. The more committed you are to the process while they are young, the less frustration you will have when they are over 6 months and still not housetrained.

Plan to be sleep deprived and inconvenienced for a short time, especially if you have a puppy under 12 weeks of age. But know that, in 30 days or less, you WILL have the reward of having a housetrained dog for the reminder of the time it shares its life with you. Which if you are lucky could be many, many years.

I promise that you will forget how much effort it took you once you no longer have to worry about stepping in pee or poop. In fact, you will be so happy that you took the time and made the effort once you are finished.

This is one instance where the work is well worth the reward!

Are you ready to dive in and get started? Great! Let's go.

Happy Housetraining!

Jenna

CHAPTER 2: WHAT EXACTLY IS HOUSETRAINING?

HOUSETRAINING IS THE PROCESS OF TEACHING OUR DOG WHERE THEIR BATHROOM IS.

"Dog's are more then happy to pee or poop exactly where they are, it's natural for them."
—JennaLee Gallicchio

Dogs don't come to us knowing how to pee and poop outside. They come to us with the knowledge that what they have always done is okay. For most dogs that means peeing and pooping right where they are the moment their bodies tell them they have to go.

Whether it is on the kitchen floor, the living room carpet or outside on the grass makes no difference to them. In understanding that your pup doesn't care where they pee or poop, just that they have to, YOU are given the POWER of teaching them where it is you want them to pee and poop.

So you see, housetraining is simply teaching your dog where it is that you want them to pee and poop. It is also giving them the tools to "tell" you that they have to go potty, when they have to go.

We will talk about this concept of a "tell" a little later, but I can say that it happens almost effortlessly as you are working through the housetraining process.

WHY TEACHING OUR DOG WHAT WE WANT IS EASIER THEN TEACHING THEM WHAT WE DON'T WANT

Let's go over this concept of teaching what we want rather than what we don't want a bit more. Do you remember when someone told you that you couldn't do something? What did you do? Well, if you are anything like me, you probably either REALLY wanted to do it or you actually did do it.

Try to associate teaching what you don't want with Pandora's Box. Sooner or later someone will be trying to open it!

If you read my book *"The Secret Of Getting Your Dog To Do What You Want"* then you are probably familiar with my training style and if you didn't, it's pretty simple.

I like to reward my dog for doing the things I want, rather than punishing the things I don't want.

Why? Because I am giving attention to both behaviors and any behaviors that receive attention are likely to continue. Since this is the case, I choose to give all of my attention to behaviors I want to happen continually.

Why waste my energy when it's not productive?

This doesn't mean ignoring a puppy who is chewing on an electrical wire or hanging on my pant leg. But even these behaviors are opportunities for me to "interrupt" what is currently happening and then "redirect" them to a behavior I do want.

For example, a puppy chewing on my pant leg, a bathrobe belt or anything else they shouldn't be chewing on is a GREAT opportunity to teach "drop-it".

All you do is get (drag your dog to the treat jar if necessary) a treat (the stinkier the better) and stick it in front of your puppy's nose. As their mouth opens to take the treat, they will simultaneously drop the object in their mouth. Say "drop-it" at the that moment they are letting it go, not before, and you are now putting a cue on the behavior of them "dropping" the forbidden object.

At some point, they will connect the "drop-it" with releasing the object (any object) that is in their mouth. Ryder was infamous for grabbing anything that dangled and tugging.

My clothes, especially my pants, have multiple holes to prove that fact. That being the case, I had an opportunity to use the technique I described above over and over again. As a result, he knows "drop-it" like a champ!

What does that example have to do with housetraining? By showing our dogs what we want over what we don't want, we give them the opportunity to be successful. The more times they are successful with any behavior, the more likely the behavior will continue to happen.

The same is true with peeing and pooping outside. The more times you get to reward peeing and pooping in the place you want them to go, the more likely they will want to do exactly that.

However, punishing the peeing and pooping for happening in the "wrong place", instead of stopping it from happening, could actually translate to it not being safe to pee and poop in FRONT OF YOU. Have you ever had a dog who went behind the couch to pee or poop? Hmmm...

Since we never really know exactly how our dog will associate what the punishment means it's easier to reward the successes and ignore the accidents. Remember, your dog is only doing what she knows. She is not trying to spite you by peeing on the floor.

WHY DO PEOPLE FAIL?

People fail because it's not the concept that we struggle with but the actual doing. Housetraining takes time and effort, there is no way around that.

You didn't learn a specific skill overnight, did you? It took repetition and practice to fully hone it and know it to where you can do it without effort or thought. The same is true for your dog and housetraining. If you have a puppy, you are also dealing with what their bodies are physically capable of doing.

Remember, a puppy's bladder muscles aren't fully developed until they are between 4 to 6 months of age.

We also fail because we forget that it's not our dogs learning housetraining but **US TEACHING** them what it means to be housetrained.

Our pups are only doing what they have been taught by their mom. They are also just doing what they have done over and over again.
Reminding ourselves of this fact will help us to re-member that, to make them successful, we have to be a consistent, patient teacher.

Giving our pups too much freedom too soon, usually just as they start to "tell" us that they have to go, is another reason we fail. When this happens, WE stop training. We think that, because they have started to let us know, they fully understand that they should pee and poop outside.

They do understand that, in the one room, but dogs don't generalize very well and need to be introduced to bigger spaces gradually, in order to learn that the same applies to each room.

Don't assume that our current dog will teach our new dog that going outside is where they go to the bathroom.

All that happens with this is that puppies follow their older siblings and think it's play time. They chase them around the yard, bounce all over, the older dog pees and the younger one watches. Then they come inside, the action stops and the puppy pees on the kitchen floor.

Some of you may have experienced this scenario and had a different outcome, but it's not the norm. In fact, I know some instances where an un-house-trained dog actually ruined the housetrained dog and both started peeing and pooping in the house.

Puppies, on the other hand, are so excited about everything and get distracted at the drop of a hat. Don't rely on your current dog's good housetraining skills to teach your new dog. It's your job to make sure the new member of the family gets it, not your dog's.

Lastly, we fail because we don't have the patience to wait for our dog to go in one spot and we take them for a walk to "get them to go".

By using a reward to get them to pee and poop (yes, a walk is a reward to your dog) we teach them that they don't have to eliminate as soon as they get outside because Mom or Dad is going to take me for a walk.

Do you really want to be walking on the days or nights during a torrential rain storm, snow storm or extreme heat? Yea, me neither.

Enough talk about failure. Let's move on to what we need to do to be successful!

CHAPTER 3:
DO THIS BEFORE YOU START

STEAM CLEAN YOUR CARPET AND BUY AN ENZYME BASED CLEANER

"Failure is the key to success; each mistake teaches us something."
—Morihei Ueshiba

Steam cleaning your carpet, especially if you have a dog who has been peeing and pooping in the house for a while, will help you to start this process with a clean slate.

If you don't fully get rid of the smell in your carpets it will be too tempting for your dog NOT to want to pee or poop in those spots. This is your first step to really setting your pup up for success.

Plus, how much more motivation will you have in wanting to keep those clean carpets free of pee and poop? It will be helpful for both of you.

Use an enzyme based cleaner (white vinegar actually works well too!) for both the steam cleaning and to clean up any accidents that happen when you start housetraining. You will want to make sure to buy a bottle before you start because accidents will happen so you may as well be prepared.

As obsessive as I was, Ryder had accidents too, so I speak from experience.

TIP:

Use warm, not hot, water with the enzyme cleaner. Hot water will kill the enzymes, making the solution useless.

There are many different enzyme based products on the market. I personally like and use white vinegar, it's less expensive and works wonderfully well, you can choose whichever one you prefer.

The most important aspect is the enzyme base. This will get rid of, rather than cover up, the urine smell. This is really important when working to teach your dog that your house is not their toilet.

Don't skip this step! Not doing it will make the housetraining process more challenging for you and your dog.

I know that steam cleaning your carpet is a big undertaking and can be expensive, but it is one step that you will not want to skip. It is that important!

CHAPTER 4: MINE!

THE REASON YOUR DOG WON'T PEE IN HIS SPACE BUT WILL PEE ALL OVER YOURS!

"There's never enough of the stuff you can't get enough of."
—Patrick H. T. Doyle

Did you know that if your dog believes that something belongs to him he won't pee or poop on it? It's true. Why, you ask?

Dogs don't pee or poop on stuff they consider to be theirs. In fact, dogs have a reflex or instinct that won't allow them to pee or poop in their territory. It's this instinct that is the drive behind the need to claim anything that ISN'T theirs.

Think of a dog you've taken for a walk, or maybe a neighbor's dog, or maybe even dogs at a dog park;

they are peeing on every fence spoke, street sign, fire hydrant or tree, basically until nothing comes out anymore.

By peeing on everything what they are actually doing is leaving a message that says, "Fido was here" and laying claim to that territory as their own.

This instinct can be a benefit when housetraining, but if you move too fast it will hurt you and your dog will be 'claiming' your house as theirs by peeing all over it.

Unless you have a puppy mill pup, who was taught to live in its own pee and poop, your dog won't pee or poop where she eats and sleeps. Why? Because, as we just talked about, dogs don't pee or poop on their stuff.

Let's talk about why it's not the same for a puppy mill pup. Puppy mill pups are forced to live, eat and sleep in their own feces and urine.

This living arrangement places them in a situation where their natural instinct has to be disregarded in order to survive.

Because of this we have to help them to reengage their natural instinct regarding their sleeping place. We do this by putting them on a strict schedule and helping them to be successful in peeing and pooping outside.

The more they poop outside of their territory, the faster this natural instinct will take over.

Does this mean that housetraining a puppy mill pup is impossible?

No, but it may mean that you will have to be a bit more diligent then someone who didn't get their pup from a pet store. Luckily, this book will help you to housetrain even the hardest case.

CHAPTER 5:
SETTING YOUR DOG UP FOR SUCCESS

FAIL TO PLAN AND PLAN TO FAIL

"By failing to prepare, you are preparing to fail."
—Benjamin Franklin

Being prepared and getting organized will take you a long way in making the housetraining process go smoothly. In this chapter I will cover the tools that you will want to use to help you set your dog up for success. Using these will ensure that your pup will want to pee and poop outside as much as you want them to.

What we will cover is:

1. Containment

2. Schedule

3. Supervision

4. The More Pees You See

5. Rewards

6. Punishment & How to use it

7. Do I Hear Bells?

This list contains the bare bones of everything you need to be successful. By the time we are finished, you are going to know exactly how to use these tools to their greatest advantage.

But first I want to explain exactly what each one means. Once we have that covered, I will tell you, step by step, how to use each one.

CONTAINMENT

By containment I mean using a Crate, X-Pen or Exercise Pen and Baby Gates, oh my! Yes, I know it seems like a lot, but each item plays its own part in the housetraining process. You can do without the X-Pen, but the crate and baby gates, in my opinion, are must haves!

Containing your pup will give you control of how much access they have to the house.

Keeping their world small—and making it larger as they get better at "holding it"will help to speed the housetraining process along—because, by containing them, we will use their natural instinct to not pee on what's theirs and teach them, inch by inch, that the house is theirs too.

CRATE

I believe that every dog should be comfortable with going into a crate. Crates are not just beneficial for housetraining but also for everyday life-for travel, for going to the groomer, if your pup needs to stay overnight at the vets.

The simple act of having your pup crate trained will help them to have less anxiety about being contained anywhere at any time.

The key to the crate is how you introduce your pup to it. You have to make them think that it is one of the best places in the world. Great stuff happens simply by them going in; closing the door happens AFTER they are comfortable going in on their own.

Follow the exercise below to get your pup to choose to go into their crate; because I not only want your pup comfortable with it, but with you putting them in there too.

You need to believe that it is a great place as well, otherwise you will be anxious-and an anxious owner can be worse than an anxious pup!

When picking out a crate, you want to make sure that you pick one that your pup will fit in when they are full size. Most crates come with a divider panel so that you can make it smaller, if necessary, when housetraining.

For some dogs you will have to make it smaller and others you won't. I left Ryder in his full sized crate and he was fine, but this is not always the case, so just be prepared. Read the product description and pick the one that will fit your dog based on weight when fully grown.

In the beginning, I wouldn't put a nice furry bed in there with them because they may just pee on that. Wait a bit for that and start off with a towel or a nice blanket you can fold up.

Remember keep, their world small in the beginning-that includes their bed.

LOVE MY CRATE!

Do this little exercise in the beginning to get them to choose to go in.

1. Bring your dog over to the crate but don't put them in.

2. Leave the door open.

3. Sprinkle the bottom of the crate with some yummy treats (use cheese, chicken, hot dogs or even beef). Leave some treats close to the entrance so your pup doesn't have to go too far to get them at first. We want to tempt them to go further in.

4. Let your pup go in; don't force but encourage your pup to go into the crate.

5. Let them clean up all the treats.

6. Repeat this exercise until your pup is going in freely.

7. After multiple attempts, your pup should start to be excited about going into their crate, looking for some more treats. When this happens, move on to the steps below.

8. Sprinkle treats in the crate.

9. Close the door when your pup is eating the treats.

10. Once your pup finishes, drop some more treats in from the top (or side if you have vari kennel) of the crate.

11. When your pup finishes and is looking to for some more, open the door and let your pup out. They may not want to come out because of all the good stuff happening. If that's the case, reward them in the crate for staying in and then end the exercise.

12. Repeat until you are able to leave your pup in there for longer and longer periods of time with the door closed.

13. Now you should be seeing your pup excited about going in and not worrying about the door closing.

If your dog seems to be anxious about the door clos- ing, go back to leaving the door open for a bit longer. Move at your dog's pace and continue to practice throughout the day.

To help continue to build the idea that the crate is where good stuff happens, you can leave them in there with some yummy stuff to occupy their time while you get some chores done.

For example, I would leave Ryder in the crate with a Kong stuffed with frozen wet dog food. It would take him forever to finish it, but it was so yummy that he paid little mind to where I was or what I was doing.

Then, when he was done, he would relax and chill out, even fall asleep, until it was time for a potty break.

I also fed him all of his meals in there. I did that to reinforce that that is where all the good stuff happens. Do the same for your puppy; it will help keep the crate a happy place.

If you have a dog for whom the crate was used as a constant, such as they were left in there almost 24 hours a day, then I would move at an even slower pace so that you can change what the crate means to them.

At this point, ALL good stuff happens in the crate. Feed her in there, water is in there. If you need to, leave them close to the front of the crate to start and gradually move them further and further in until they are at the back of the crate.

You can do this over a period of a week, or longer if necessary.

You don't want to close the door on her, but she has to choose to go in there to get what she wants out.

Once she starts to trust that you won't force her in and then lock her up, she will let down her guard.

It's at this point you can start the exercise of slowly building up her being okay with the door shut.

For a dog like this you would use the crate in conjunction with an X-Pen. Place the crate as one of the X-Pen panels and leave the crate door open all the time.

Drop yummy treats close to the entrance of the crate door, then in the middle and then at the back.

X-PEN OR EXERCISE PEN

A great way to use the X-Pen is in conjunction with the crate. The crate is used when you can't be there to supervise the choices your pup is making. An X-Pen gives them some room to roam in when you are there to supervise.

Remember, the key to being successful with house-training is by keeping your pup's world small and *gradually* making it larger.

An X-Pen, or an Exercise Pen, is a gated enclosure that does not have a top or bottom. Most of them are made of durable wire, have eight panels, one being a gate, and are two feet in width. They come in different heights starting at 23 inches and go up to 48 inches.

Although I like exercise pens, I believe they should be used together with a crate, not in place of a crate. A crate teaches our pups that they have to respect a barrier. If they jump on the walls they don't move, there is a top so they can't jump out.

With an x-pen, if a dog gets restless they can jump on the walls and possibly even jump out. I've seen dogs climb over the walls; puppies will get very creative in their desire to explore. Ryder did it when I bought him one.

Again, I am not saying that you shouldn't use one. I am just saying that it has its disadvantages if used alone and doesn't do as good a job of containing your pup as a crate will.

I know that there are some, possibly even you reading this now, who feel that an X-Pen is more humane. But the truth is, it is all in the teaching. Mattie loved his crate and Ryder puts himself to sleep in his at times. Emmy on the other hand I had to work on the crate with but she will tolerate it. I say this only because every dog is different.

An exercise pen comes in handy once your pup understands and respects the boundaries of the wire walls. I work with a Cane Corso who is over 100lbs and he goes into his brother's X-Pen; his brother is a 15lb Havenese.

Though he does occasionally try to walk through the panels, for the most part he respects the boundary that it presents.

BABY GATES

Once you start to see your pup becoming more and more successful, you will want to start making their world bigger. Using baby gates allows us to do this gradually so that they can be successful in other parts of the house as well.

If you have children you can definitely see where I am going with this, but if you don't you may be struggling just a bit. Baby Gates serve the same purpose as the crate and the x-pen; they contain your dog but allow you to control how much access to the house they have.

We want our pups to be able to explore and have more freedom; we just want to make sure we are not making their world too large too fast. That is just asking to have that 'pee on what's not mine' instinct kick in and we don't want that happening.

When picking a baby gate, I would advise against picking a wooden one without a door. You will spend a lot of your time stepping over it which can become a pain. Definitely invest in one with a door. You will be thankful you did.

There are many on the market today that are held in place by pressure-mount systems that won't need to be permanently fixed to the wall. So installation is actually very easy.

TETHERING

Tethering, or tying your pup to you, is another method that can be used in containing your pup. It is also a great method to use along with the other methods because it exposes your pup to the rest of your house but she is under complete supervision and can't get into trouble.

Keep your pup on leash and wrap the leash around your waist-or link through a pant belt loop-and then tie it into a knot. Make sure the knot isn't too tight since you want to be able to untie it at some point.

This method allows you to keep an eye on your pup, get some tasks accomplished and gets your pup some exercise all the while under your complete supervision.

This does not guarantee that they will not pee or poop in your presence–you still have to watch them for the telltale signs that have to go–it just guarantees that they remain in your sight.

This way requires bit more attention and effort on your part, but it will work.

SCHEDULE

A schedule will be one of your most valuable tools, if not your *most* valuable tool. It is THAT important. By keeping a schedule, you will know exactly when your pup has to go pee and poop, when any accidents are happening, and how long your pup is actually able to "hold it".

Keeping and sticking to a schedule will help to identify any weak links, especially if you have more than one person in the house helping with the housetraining process. An example can be found in the appendix.

RECORD KEEPING

Think of housetraining as your job for the next 30 days. By keeping track of your progress, you will have a clear picture of what is happening, which is why the most important step of the schedule is to put it in writing.

Being accountable is a big part of housetraining. It is up to us to make sure that we are doing the RIGHT things and that these actions are teaching our pups to pee and poop in the RIGHT place.

You want to know when your dog eats (breakfast, lunch and dinner), how much water they are drinking, when and where they are peeing and when they are pooping. Keep track of the successes and the accidents.

By knowing this information you are setting yourself up to have advance notice of what your pup will be doing and when. Ultimately, it's this information that will give you the upper hand and make the housetraining easier.

I know that, initially, this sounds like a lot of work for everyone who is involved, but, by keeping track in writing, there will be no question of what exactly your pup has been up because it will be there for all to see.

You can find an example of a schedule and record keeping in the appendix. Get yours ready for the next 30 days. Any pre-work that you can do in advance is one less thing for you to do during. It will keep the process moving smoothly and help you to feel less overwhelmed.

As for the actual times and such, there is flexibility and you can fit it into your lifestyle. Just remember, a younger puppy will need to go out more often, so expect that you may be a bit sleep deprived for the first week or two.

If your puppy sleeps through the night then that's a bonus, but expecting the worst will have you prepared.

MID-DAY VISITS

Mid-Day Visits will help you to keep your pup on schedule. If you are working during the day, and most of us are, plan to come home for lunch, ask a neighbor, sibling, or hire a pet sitter/dog walker to come in to let your pup out.

You will want to do this especially if you are going to be away for more than 4 hours and if your puppy is between 8 and 16 weeks old.

Remember, your puppy's bladder isn't fully developed until between the ages of 4 to 6 months. So them getting a mid-day potty break will help them not have to pee or poop in their space-making both of you happy.

If you can't do this, then expect accidents to happen during the day. Just know that it won't stop or hurt the process and be prepared to have to clean them really well when you get home. This is where your enzyme based cleaner will come in extremely handy.

SUPERVISION

You will want to supervise, supervise, supervise your pup. Did I mention that you want to supervise? The more you are in their presence and watching them, the better off you will both be and the more pees you will get to witness, which will increase your success rate.

When you are supervising your pup, you get the opportunity to see what their signals are. By signals, I mean their pre-pee and pre-poop dance. They can vary from dog to dog, but they are usually pretty similar and the dance ALWAYS precedes the pee and the poop.

THE PRE-PEE DANCE

The pee dance is a series of steps that usually involves sniffing while walking and then a squat. Once the squat happens, the dance is over and at that point you now have a pool of pee somewhere you didn't want it.

What does this mean for you? That your job is to catch the sniffing and add to the dance.

How? Easy!

When you see your pup sniffing and walking, ask them if they have to go out. This is now step 2, instead of the squatting step. Before going outside, put a leash on and grab a yummy treat to reward a successful pee.

TRAINING TIP:

Keeping your pup on a leash will help to keep them from associating going outside to mean playing in the big, exciting world. Going out means to go potty, not to play. If your pup plays BEFORE peeing or pooping they will forget why they came out in the first place and pee when they get back inside. Playing is a reward for going potty, not the other way around.

When you get outside, bring your pup to where you want them to pee. Stand still as you wait for them to reengage the dance.

Don't be surprised if your pup gets distracted. She's a puppy–that's expected! Just stand there quietly and wait. If you move to speed up the process, instead of helping them to find a place you are actually giving them another distraction–YOU. So stay still and wait.

If you didn't guess it yet, your step is to wait for them, by being quiet and still, to re-initiate the pee dance. When they start sniffing and walking, not pouncing or playing, you know it's happened. Continue to stay quiet and still at this point; let them do the work.

When your dog squats and starts to pee, you will want to put a 'cue' to this action. For example, I like "Hurry-up". No, it's not polite, but there are times I really want Ryder to hurry-up so I can go inside. Like on those super hot, rainy, or cold days.

You can use whatever you'd like, but here are a few to choose from: "pee", "go pretty", "potty". If you don't like any of those, pick your own, but definitely pick something. It can be anything. The word will take on the meaning of peeing as you pair it with the action of peeing.

The word is not important but having a dog pee on command can be extremely convenient.

Say the cue softly, followed by a soft "Good Boy". The reason I say softly is because some dogs get interrupted very easily and will stop mid-stream. This is really a pain because then you have to start the entire dance over. So speak softly and be monotone.

When your pup is finished, this is when you get excited, very excited. Have a party! This is the biggest and best thing your pup has EVER done!

Then give them the treat and have another party. Your goal is to end the dance with them wanting to do it over and over!

THE PRE-POOP DANCE

The poop dance is very similar to the pee dance, with a few variations. The poop dance usually involves circling-very rarely will it contain sniffing, though it is possible, so be on the lookout for that too- which is then followed by a curving of the body.

The curving includes legs close together with their back rounded. Again, once the curving of the body happens, the dance is over and at you now have a pile of poop somewhere you didn't want it.

At this point, your job is exactly the same as in the pre-pee dance. Catch the circling and add a new step. When you see your pup circling, you again ask them if they have to go out. Step 2 again becomes go out instead of curving.

Again, remember to put her on a leash and grab a yummy treat before heading out.

As before, the same rules apply to playing. Playing is a reward for pooping and it shouldn't be used to encourage the pooping. You're outside already be-cause your pup TOLD you, by circling, that they HAVE to poop.

Again, bring them to where you want them to poop. Stand still as you wait for them to reengage the dance. Again, don't be surprised if your pup gets dis-tracted. She's a puppy! Just stand quietly and wait.

Once your pup starts to circle, the dance has begun again, wait and, as they curve their body, you will want to put a different 'cue' to this action.

Here are another few examples, but again the word is not as important as using something. "Poop", "go pretty", "potty"- you can use any of these as long as you haven't used them as your cue word to initiate peeing.

Same as before, you will want to say the cue softly, followed by a soft "Good boy". We don't want to interrupt, so remember to say it softly while being monotone.

Poop on the ground and your pup is finished? You know what to do! Have a party!

THE "TELL"

As the two of you get better at the Pre-Pee and Pre-Poop dances, your pup will actually add another step. This step will be a completely different signal to let you know they have to go out.

I call this a "Tell" and the "Tell" is exactly what it sounds like. Your dog is TELLING you they have to go out. It's your job to catch it. This is sometimes very challenging because we aren't always looking for it.

Some tells to look for are going to the door and staring at it. They may even stare at you. Usually staring at the door happens first. Ryder did this; he also followed it with a whine if I wasn't paying attention and when he fully understood that his bathroom was outside.

Others may offer a small bark or a whine, but I wouldn't look for this one just yet. The whining or barking is usually the very last tell that happens and only when they are completely housetrained.

Pay attention to your dog because he could be offering something completely different than what I have mentioned above. But he will be "Telling" you something.

When this starts to happen, you can celebrate a bit. Your hard work is definitely paying off!

THE MORE PEES YOU SEE

The more pees you see happen will help to shorten the time that it takes to teach your pup to pee outside.

If you can see 99% of pees happening outside, then your percentage of success has sky rocketed and the amount of time it takes to housetrain your pup has decreased.

In order to do this you have to become a bit, okay a lot, obsessive about the pre-pee and pre-poop dances. I was taking Ryder out every 15 minutes for a while, until he was telling me that he had to go.

Yes, that seems completely excessive and part of me would agree with you, but I had the time available and it was what he required.

To put this in a bit more context, I brought Ry home at the beginning of summer. He was playing non-stop with his new big brother, Mattie, and because of this, I didn't limit his water. Because I didn't limit his water and he was constantly drinking and playing, that meant he had to pee A LOT!

More than I even thought he would. But because I was waiting too long and he was having accidents, I had to bring him out more frequently.

So though my circumstances may seem overly obsessive, the point of my story is to let you know that you have to do whatever is needed in order to help your pup be successful.

It could be every 15 minutes or it could be every hour. Your schedule will help you to figure out what is right for your pup.

Your goal is to see 99% of pees and poops. Every pee that happens without you witnessing, ie. accidents, will require 10 more witnessed by you just to get your pup back on the successful housetraining track. 99% is the optimal goal, but if you can't do that, don't worry, you will still get your pup house-trained.

How long it takes will just be your variable.

REWARDS

Rewarding your dog for peeing and pooping outside is a MUST! What you choose to use for a reward is up to you, and most importantly, your dog.

Verbal praise and a petting party will work for some dogs. Treats and then play time will work for others. Whatever you choose is fine. The key is that your **dog has to enjoy it**. It's not about what you think they should like, but what your dog actually likes.

You will know your reward is working based on your dog's reaction. If they keep going to the bathroom outside, just to make "it" happen–it's working!

PUNISHMENT AND HOW TO EFFECTIVELY USE IT

We talked about teaching your dog what you want instead of punishing what you don't want. But I know, sometimes, taking away something the dog wants to get them to do what we want can help the process to move along. I will explain in just a bit how I do this and when I use it.

I don't yell at my dog for peeing or pooping in the house, especially after the fact. Yelling at your dog will only scare them. It's also hard to say if your dog will associate you being angry with them for peeing and pooping or you just being scary.

It can even make them hide what they do from you. Think about the poop behind the couch...hmm. It can also make going to the bathroom in front of you not safe. This is a HUGE problem when trying to housetrain.

I fostered a dog who had been yelled at for peeing and pooping and getting her to go in front of me, on leash, took a LONG time! Don't make this mistake.

My yelling is actually just a loud noise, such as a clap or a loud "HEY" that I hope will startle my pup mid-stream to interrupt the flow. If I can stop the flow of pee coming from their bodies, then I can take them outside to get it right.

If that doesn't work (and with my pup Emmy it didn 't!) then I just clean up the mess with them out of the way without having a "bad puppy/dog" dialog. It was my mistake, not theirs.

No rubbing their noses in it! If poop happens, poop happens. It is your responsibility to make sure it doesn't happen, that's why you are reading this book. Rubbing your dog's nose in it is another way to scare them.

It doesn't teach them anything except that you can't be trusted. Don't do that to your pup or yourself.

You can actually use not being able to hang out with you as a form of punishment. Our pups always want to be in the action. When we are keeping their world small, YOU are the action. So getting to spend time with you is fun.

If you use it as a privilege for making good choices regarding housetraining, it can help to move the process along.

I only use this type of time-out after my pup really, really likes their crate, but it works great for teaching them that if they don't pee, that they don't get to be part of the action. Do this when you know it's time for your pup to be going to the bathroom and they are not focusing or unable to focus.

After about 5 minutes of being outside with no luck, come back in and put him in his crate for about 15 minutes. Set a timer so you don't forget. Continue until they potty outside.

Using this form of punishment helps your pup to pay attention to what their body is telling them and makes it a bit easier next time you take them out to pee and poop.

Remember, less movement from both you and your pup helps them to focus and heed their body's signals. It is very easy for them to get distracted by different scents and movements. Housetraining in the fall with the blowing leaves is definitely not fun!

DO I HEAR BELLS?

So many people ask me, "How do I get my dog to bark at me to tell me they have to go out?" My response is always that I don't know; my dogs don't bark at me as a sign that they have to go out and honestly I like it that way.

I don't like a dog barking at me and telling me to do something. In my opinion, it is the equivalent to a person yelling at me and I don't like that either.

Teaching a dog to bark at you and you complying gives them a really annoying tool that makes you do what they want just to get them to stop. So my suggestion is to not teach your dog to bark at you but to teach them how to ring a bell!

By teaching your dog that ringing a bell equals going out, you get the signal you want and they have a way to tell you that you understand. It is a win, win.

Just remember the bell is for peeing and pooping only, NOT play!

If you take them out to play when they ring the bell, how often do you think they will be ringing the bell? All the time? Yup. I would too if something fun happened every time I did it. So be very diligent that ringing the bell equals potty time and not playtime.

Teaching your dog to ring the bell is easy. First step is to get a bell for them to ring. You can use any bell and a piece of string or a shoe lace. Just make sure the bells you choose are light enough for your dog to push but loud enough for you to hear.

Jingle bells or a cow bell are actually both good choices.

Once you have the bell, you want to hang it next to a door. If you hang it on the door, the bells will ring every time someone comes in.

Since we want that sound to mean going out to your dog, hanging it next to the door is the best idea, otherwise it will lose its effectiveness.

To teach your dog to ring the bell, simply follow the exercise below. Do this exercise at a time that is NOT potty time. That's just asking for an accident.

1. Encourage your pup to touch it with his nose by holding it in your hand.

2. As the bell rings, praise and give a treat.

3. Encourage your pup to repeat it a few times, always praising and treating as you do.

4. Stop holding the bell and encourage your pup to touch it as it's hanging on the wall.

5. Once he does, praise, treat. Great job!

Next potty break, encourage your dog to ring the bell BEFORE you go outside and do it every time until your pup is ringing the bell on their own. Just remember, the bell is for peeing, not playing or walking.

I can't say this enough..don't make the mistake of letting it be for play because your pup will be trying to get you out a lot and it won't be going because they have to go to the bathroom.

One of the bonuses using this technique, is that you can bring the bells anywhere with you and that gives your dog a way to tell you they have to go wherever you are.

CHAPTER 6: FREE REIN

LETTING YOUR DOG EARN RIGHTS TO THE HOUSE

"A happy life is one spent in learning, earning, and yearning."
—Lillian Gish

Our ultimate goal with housetraining is that we have a dog we can trust not to pee or poop in our house. More importantly, they are able to tell us when they do have to go out.

Rushing this process and giving our pups too much freedom to soon will back fire on us, so you want to make sure that you start their world out small and make it bigger **slowly**.

Why? By allowing our pup to gradually have more space you, are teaching them that your space is their space. Remember that little instinct of theirs to pee on anything they don't consider theirs? This practice helps to teach them to learn, inch by inch, that it is their house too.

Once you are on a schedule with pee and poop is happening outside consistently and your pup is starting to tell you they have to go out to do their business, it is time to make their world a bit larger.

Initially, their world was their crate and their X-Pen, now it's time to make it their crate, X-Pen and another room. Here is where those baby gates will come in handy!

When introducing another room, you will want to make sure that you block off the door that exits from the new room and enters into a room that isn't allowed. For example, the crate and X-Pen have been in the kitchen but your pup hasn't had free access to the kitchen. Put the baby gate in the door that has access to the living room or dining room so that your pup has to stay in the kitchen.

If you have more than one entrance/exit, you will want more than one baby gate. This is important. Giving your dog too much freedom before he believes that the current room is his, you are only asking for that instinct to kick in.

The tortoise, not the hare, wins the race. Slow and steady is the pace. When in the new room, go back to supervising a bit more closely. We want only successful encounters when entering a new place. So keep an eye on them and look for any pre-dance signals.

A tip might be to take them out for a potty break just before introducing the new space. As they get more reliable in the new space, add another room, and another, and another, and another, until you re-alize that they have free rein and roam of the house.

As a side note, when introducing carpeted rooms, move slowly because rugs and grass can be easily confused. You can do this by using an X-Pen to move a little bit at a time on the carpeted surface. I would start with hard surface floors, like tile, wood or linoleum, first. Also makes clean up a bit easier.

If you only have carpets, no worries, you can get creative. Go to your local hardware/flooring store and purchase some linoleum flooring pieces so you can put them over the carpet. Then introduce your pup to the carpeted areas gradually.

CHAPTER 7: GETTTING STARTED

APPLYING THE TOOLS WE TALKED ABOUT

"Tools are only as good as your use of them, so make sure to use them fully."
—JennaLee Gallicchio

By this time, you should have all of the tools we talked about.

1. White Vinegar or an enzymed based cleaner and a clean carpet.

2. Crate, X-Pen, Baby Gates.

3. A schedule all ready to be followed.

4. Recording sheet posted for all to see and markdown on the refrigerator.

5. Your bells (If you are using them).

6. Treats for rewarding.

7. Pee and Poop cue words. ("Hurry up", "Pee", "Poop", "Go Pretty", etc.).

Now we are ready to put this whole housetraining thing into action.

Are you excited? You should be; this is the beginning of you with a housetrained dog.

We know what that means, right? A house free of pee and poop! YAY!

Here is what you will want to do once you have noticed the pre-pee or pre-poop dance, or it's just time to take your puppy out because the schedule says so.

There are two examples of what to do if your pup doesn't go potty and what to do when they do.

EXAMPLE 1:
DOESN'T PEE OR POOP

1. Put their leash on (4 to 6 foot leash rather than a retractable—allows for to much freedom and easy distraction).

2. If using a bell, encourage them to ring it before going outside.

3. Take your pup to their pee and poop space.

4. Stand quietly and wait for them to go. (Remember, your job is to not be another distraction).

5. Pup DOESN'T go potty.

6. **DON'T TAKE FOR A WALK** (A walk is a reward for a job well done, Not to try and make them go).

7. Move to a different spot a few feet from where you are.

8. Wait a few minutes (3 or so).

9. Bring them in and put them in their crate or pen.

10. Set a timer for 10 to 15 minutes and repeat. (some dogs will be quicker, while others are longer–adjust the time as needed).

11. Write down the series of events on your Potty Record.

EXAMPLE 2: PUP DOES PEE OR POOP

1. Put their leash on (4 to 6 foot leash rather than a retractable—allows for to much freedom and easy distraction).

2. If using a bell, encourage them to ring it before going outside.

3. Take your pup to their pee and poop space.

4. Stand quietly and wait for them to go. (Remember, your job is to not be another distraction).

5. Your Pup pees or poops.

6. **Quietly** say your Pee or Poop Cue word and then 'Good boy, Good girl'. Repeat until they are finished.

7. Have a party (verbally praise make it a PARTY! It's supposed to be exciting.) AND give a tasty treat.

8. Write down the series of events on your Potty Record.

9. Have some play time or go for a walk.

Chapter 8: HOUSETRAINING FAQ'S

CHALLENGES THAT CAN COME WITH THE TERRITORY

When we are teaching dogs anything, there is always the challenge of each dog being unique. Because of this, not all dogs fit the same mold. When it 's your dog that doesn't follow the norm, it can really poke a hole in your sail.

For that reason, I have included challenges that some of my clients have experienced. This will help you to get over any humps and to know that you are not the only one.

Q: I have multiple dogs; will this work for me?

A: Absolutely! Here are some mistakes that are common with a multiple dog household:

Letting them ALL go outside *without* supervision.

I cannot stress enough how important witnessing your dog going to the bathroom outside is. If you are not seeing the pees and poops happen before you let your dogs back in, you can almost depend on having to clean up a mess in the house.

Letting them ALL go out together.

Puppies get distracted easily and are always looking for the next play thing. Taking them out individually and witnessing them pee and poop will go a long way to getting them housetrained. I know that, in the beginning, it will be a lot of work but when it's done, it's done. In the long run, it is the easiest way to get your ultimate goal accomplished.

Having more than one dog is triple the trouble. Yes, I meant triple.

It's a lot more work than most people ever bargain for. Follow the plan for each dog, and take them out separately to start. Once they begin to understand the concept–that going outside is pee time–then you can start taking them out together.

Remember this is only for 30 days and, once your pups are housetrained, you will never have to worry about this again. You can do it!

Q: My dog eats his poop!?

A: As disgusting as this habit is, it's actually very common for dogs to do this.

In fact, puppies are taught this at a very young age from their mothers, since keeping the 'den' area clean will keep away predators. Most puppies will grow out of this. For the ones that don 't, there are a few things to know.

The technical term is "coprophagia." This is a behavioral issue that is influenced by diet. Try adding pineapple to your pup's diet. Pineapple tastes great going in but not so good coming out. I've had multiple clients have success with this technique.

You will find some other stool-eating deterrents if you do a bit of research, talk to your vet, or you can do some online research as well for some ideas, if the pineapple doesn't work.

If nothing works, take your pup to the Veterinarian to have them tested. They may be missing some essential minerals or suffer from some type of deficiency such as EPI or Exocrine Pancreatic Insufficiency.

Either way, make sure you clean up the poop because some dogs have been known to eat the poop if it's still there regardless.

Q: Nothing I do is working!

If nothing you do seems to be working, look at these questions and answer honestly for yourself. If you are not following through somewhere, that could be your weak spot.

Make that correction and start over. Remember, these tools and instructions are only as good as you are in utilizing them.

- Are you keeping a schedule?

- Are you writing all of the pee and poop successes AND accidents down?

This will help you to identify times when your dog is going so that you can get better at predicting when they will have to go.

- Is each person doing their part and writing down what the dog is doing during each potty break?

- Are you containing your pup or are you giving them free rein of the house?

- Are you witnessing the pees and poops or are you letting your dog out by themselves?

This will sabotage you, especially if you have more than one dog. Witnessing the pees and poops in the beginning is crucial. Otherwise your dog is outside running around, not eliminating. Once done running, they come in, hear their body, and pee or poop inside.

- Are you supervising?

- Are you catching the pre-pee and pre-poop dance?

- Are you free feeding (leaving the food out so your pup can eat at any time) or are you adhering to the scheduled times for all of their meals?

Free feeding WILL sabotage your efforts. Keep to the schedule. If your pup is a picky eater, don't worry, they will eat at scheduled times once they realize that there is nothing available until the next meal time. I promise you that your dog will not starve himself.

- Did you stop following the schedule too soon or when your dog just started to be reliable?

- Did you make their world too big too soon?

- Did you answer yes to most of these?

If so it may be time to take your pup to the Veterinarian to have them checked. Sometimes it's not us doing anything wrong, but something wrong with our dog.

A sick dog cannot be expected to hold it. So please make sure that your dog is fully healthy before continuing with a strict house-training plan.

If you get a clean bill of health and still nothing is working, it may be time to call in a professional. Sometimes an objective third party can help us to see what step we are missing.

Q: Why does my dog keep peeing on my area rugs?

A: Area rugs fall under the same category as carpeting and it is easy for some dogs to confuse this with grass.

Something you can consider is steam cleaning the area rug or throwing it in the washer if it's small. (Remember to use white vinegar or an enzyme based cleaner). You can also pour some white vinegar on the spot and let it dry. This will also help to get rid of the pee/poop scent.

Making the area rug a play place with supervision, after a successful potty break, is a great way to show your pup that that rug is their property too. Use their natural instinct to your benefit whenever possible.

Q: How do I get my dog to bark at me to go outside?

A: I addressed this bad habit a little when talking about teaching our dogs to ring a bell, but it bears repeating because so many people want to be told by their dogs that they have to go out.

As I said, my dogs don't bark at me as a way of letting me know they have to go out and that's the way I like it. They do "Tell" me they have to go out but they do it in other ways-much quieter ways.

Ask anyone who has a dog who barks at them constantly and they will tell you that you will regret encouraging this later.

Teach your dog to ring a bell—this is a great way for them to tell you. If you choose not to use a bell, look for these signs:

Sniffing or Circling

Remember that the pee/poop dance is the very first "Tell" that you get. Catch this and get your pup out.

Going to the Door

This was Ryder's and Emmy's first "Tell". I think it's the most common one you just have to really be paying attention. If you know their schedule you will know what this means when they do it.

Staring

My dog Mattie did this intently and wouldn't leave until I asked, "Do you have to go out?" Ryder and Emmy have both started this one too, although he is not as intent as Mattie was so I have to be really paying attention.

Whining

If our dogs have been doing any of the above "Tells" and we haven't been listening this could be the FINAL one before they go in the house. I had an experience where Ryder did this, but because we had already gone out about a half hour earlier and he did pee and poop, I ignored him.

That was a mistake as he started pooping on my carpet. Being that he did tell me, and I didn't listen, I had no one to blame but myself.

These are the easiest ways to have your dog "Tell" you they have to go out. Trust me when I say that barking is not the way that you will want to go.

Barking is a very powerful tool for a dog and, once they find out that it works, it is not one that is easy to get rid of.

Most dogs don't stop barking but get louder and louder in their effort to get your attention. Most people I know cave in to their dogs bark way before the dog stops.

My sister's dog, Sammy, was a barker and he taught her to go to the kitchen to get him cookies. It worked like a charm and my sister was very well trained!

Q: What if my dog is marking in the house?

A: When a dog starts marking in the house I always try to figure out a few things first and I usually start by asking these questions:

- Has anything changed in the house? If so, what?

- Did you move?

- Did you get a new puppy or new dog who is having accidents?

- Did you have a pup who was telling you every time they had to go out or were they still having accidents?

Figuring out what could've possibly triggered it will help in getting the problem solved faster. As always check with your Veterinarian to get your pup a clean bill of health. Then be prepared to put them back on a while and take away some freedoms too. Remember your pup needs to understand that the proper place for the them to go is outside, not inside.

The bottom line is this: if they are peeing or pooping inside, they don't fully understand and you need to make it very clear to them where their bathroom is.

Make sure that you have thoroughly cleaned up any place that any of the marking has happened using an enzyme based cleaner.

While you are trying to re-teach them use a bellyband, or a piece of cloth such as an ace bandage, that wraps around and covers their urethra. This doesn't stop them from peeing but makes it uncomfortable because they are peeing on themselves.

A dog who was previously housetrained (no accidents for 6 months or more (not including being sick) and told you they had to go by giv-ing one or multiple, of the above tells) will get this really quickly and the marking will stop once they understand that the consequence of going inside is peeing on themselves.

If you have a dog who wasn't housetrained it will take longer, how long will depend on how consistent you are. I would go for the full 30 days and start the program all over.

If you moved you should start the training pro-gram again. Dogs don't generalize from house to house. Housetrained in one house DOES NOT equal housetrained in another house. This a common mistake that many people make. Your pup hasn't learned the concept presented in the "Mine" chapter yet.

A new un-housetrained dog or puppy can un-train a housetrained puppy. Put them both on a strict housetraining schedule. Both will most likely pick it up faster as the previously house-trained dog remembers the routine. Have pa-tience and be consistent.

Housetraining is a process. Follow the steps with every new dog and in any new environ-ment and you will be successful. It is one of the most challenging times you will have with your pup but you can do it!

Q: Why is my older dog is starting to have accidents?

A: An older dog who has accidents is part of having a senior dog. Again you will want to make sure that nothing other than old age is the issue and have your pup examined by your Veterinarian. If he gets a clean bill of health then there are just a few things to understand.

If your pup was successfully housetrained then they are probably letting you know that they need to go out more frequently. Start to trust that they know their bodies and most likely can't hold it, even if they have held in the past for extended periods of time. ***This is not housetraining breaking down, it is just your pup getting older.***

If your pup has never successfully been house-trained then you may want to put them on a strict schedule to help get them fully trained. Just don't expect for them to be able to hold it like a younger dog would be able to.

The same is true for bladder problems. If your pup has a weak bladder you can't expect them to hold it like a healthy pup.

You can teach them to use a wee-wee pad by following the steps in this book. The only dif-ference is that you would back track. Bring a wee-wee pad outside and bring your pup to pee on it. Once they understand that that is where they should be going then bring the pad inside. Take them to the pad inside, instead of bringing them outside, and reward when they go pee or poop on it. Definitely use treats here.

An aging dog is a part of life and sooner or later our dogs bodies will start digressing. Just love your pup and have patience with them.

Q: What if I want my dog to pee and poop in a certain area of my yard?

A: This is actually very easy to do. Pick the area you want them to go and make it distinct. By this I mean put up a little fence for the full area you want them to use. Something as simple as a garden fence that you stick into the ground by hand will work.

Once the area is marked off cover the ground with pebbles or mulch, sand will work too, to really help your pup differentiate and understand that this is their spot. You can leave the space with just grass but the more distinct you make it the easier it will be for you pup.

If you have more than one pup you plan on letting them use the spot, definitely take that into account when you pick how big or small you want the area to be.

Now that you have the spot all set up your job is to bring your dog there EVERY TIME you take them out. This is where they go, no where else. If you make an exception some-times so will your dog.

Follow the same steps that you used when they do or don't pee.

This may be a bit challenging for a puppy that has to go when they have to go, but will work beautifully as their bladder muscles are devel-oping.

Q: My dog is a constant repeat offender, so will this work?

A: If you have repeat offender, or a dog who was making progress but continues to have accidents in the house "sometimes," then this can definitely work for you. You should start from scratch by going back to the beginning and not allowing your dog to have free rein of your house UNLESS SUPERVISED.

This is really important. You already know that if your dog is left to their own devices they will make bad choices. Don't give them the oppor-tunity. Use this program and follow it exactly as it's listed.

You will also want to make sure that you steam clean any areas that have been favorite spots for your dog to pee or poop in. Know that teaching your dog to be completely housetrained, and to be trusted in your home unsupervised, may take you a year.

It could happen sooner, but don't rush it! Remember, this was where you went wrong in your multiple attempts to housetrain your pup before. Be the tortoise in this process and not the hare. SLOW AND STEADY is your game. That is the only way this can work for you.

CHAPTER 9:
YOU ARE ON YOUR WAY

STAY THE COURSE FOR THE NEXT 30 DAYS

"Stay the course."
—John Gresham Machen

This book gives you every tool you need to successfully housetrain your dog in 30 days or less. Your only requirement is to stay the course and apply each tool fully.

How fast or how slow is you move is unimportant. What is important is how consistent you are being and how many pees you are witnessing. In order to do that:

1. Be diligent and consistent. Once your dog is housetrained you will never have to do this again! Once housetrained–ALWAYS housetrained.

2. Start your pup's world small and slowly increase it. Remember your pup's instinct to claim what isn't theirs.

3. Don't stop too soon! Err on the side of being over diligent. Be obsessive.

4. Follow these guidelines **exactly**.

5. Have patience! Housetraining is a time consuming process, have patience with your pup and yourself. You will have accidents, we all do. Just know an accident or two, or three, doesn't equal failure. It is just a setback.

6. You can do it! I know that if I can do it, you can do it. I believe in you.

Remind yourself over and over that once you have successfully housetrained your dog, you will never have to do this again. It will help you to get through any moments of frustration you will most likely have.

If you find yourself with a challenge that I didn't address here, please feel free to contact me directly at Jenna@AllStarPaws.com and I will be more than happy to help you.

I also offer a Housetraining Bootcamp online training program and support program. These are helpful if you feel like you need someone to be accountable to. I have given you all the tools you need in this book but sometimes having someone walk the journey with you is comforting.

If you are interested in the online program or support you can find them at: AllStarPawsAcademy.com

APPENDIX

HOUSETRAINING SCHEDULE EXAMPLE

This is a housetraining schedule based on the needs of a healthy four-month-old puppy. Vary this schedule as needed according to your schedule and the age/needs of your puppy or adult dog.

Again if you can't take care of all your pup's needs due to your work schedule or other conflicts, consider asking or hiring someone to help you. Following this schedule closely will help move the housetraining process along smoothly and efficiently. Remember "The More Pees You See" guideline.

Make your own record keeping schedule (found below the time schedule) and adjust times as needed. List any others you think might be helpful but keep the day/time, meal, who and what the puppy did and where.

Keep the schedule on the fridge to help keep track of who took the puppy out and what the puppy did. This will help everyone to be on the same page. It is also a great way to keep track of when the accidents are happening which will make fixing the problem much easier.

Time	Action
7:00 am Wake up	Immediately take your pup outside. Usually the easiest pee of the day.
7:30 am Breakfast	Feed your pup in crate and give some water.
7:45 am Morning walk	Take your pup out 15 minutes after eating to pee and poop. The food pushing on their bladders will help to make this an easy one.
11:00 am	Play, potty, and then take a walk after peeing and/or pooping.
11:15 am Lunch	Feed your pup in their crate and give some water.
11:45 AM	Potty break.
2:30 PM	Play, potty, and then take a walk after peeing and/or pooping.
4:00 PM	Potty break.
5:30 pm Dinner	Feed your pup in their crate and give some water.
5:45 PM	Potty break.
7:00 PM	Play, potty, and then take a walk after peeing and/or pooping.
8:00 PM	Remove water.
Middle of night	Potty break if necessary.

RECORD KEEPING SCHEDULE

Keeping records of every meal, pee and poop successes and accidents seems a bit overwhelming but the better organized you are the easier this will be. You can do it! Just think in 30 days or less this will all be worth it.

Day/Time	Meal	Who	What Puppy Did
Monday 7am		Mom	(peed, pooped, did nothing, outside, paper, accident on floor, etc.)
Monday 7:30am	Breakfast	Mom	
Monday 7:45am		Mom	Peed and pooped outside

YOU CAN RING MY BELL!

TEACH YOUR PUP TO RING A BELL EXERCISE

To teach your dog to ring the bell, simply follow the exercise below. Do this exercise at a time that is NOT potty time. That's just asking for an accident.

- Encourage your pup to touch it with his nose by holding it in your hand.

- As the bell rings, praise and give a treat.

- Encourage your pup to repeat it a few times, always praising and treating as you do.

- Stop holding the bell and encourage your pup to touch it as it's hanging on the wall.

- Once he does, praise, treat. Great job!

Next potty break, encourage your dog to ring the bell BEFORE you go outside and do it every time until your pup is ringing the bell on their own. Just remember, the bell is for peeing, not playing or walking.

I can't say this enough..don't make the mistake of letting it be for play because your pup will be trying to get you out a lot and it won't be going because they have to go to the bathroom.

LEARNING TO DANCE

PRE-POOP AND PRE-PEE DANCE STEPS

The steps are easy but you have to learn to apply them. Here is what to do if your pup doesn't go potty and what to do when they do.

EXAMPLE 1: DOESN'T PEE OR POOP

- Put their leash on (4 to 6 foot leash rather than a retractable—allows for to much freedom and easy distraction).

- If using a bell, encourage them to ring it before going outside.

- Take your pup to their pee and poop space.

- Stand quietly and wait for them to go. (Remember, your job is to not be another distraction).

- Pup DOESN'T go potty.

- **DON'T TAKE FOR A WALK** (A walk is a reward for a job well done, Not to try and make them go).

- Move to a different spot a few feet from where you are.

- Wait a few minutes (3 or so).

- Bring them in and put them in their crate or pen.

- Set a timer for 10 to 15 minutes and repeat. (some dogs will be quicker, while others are longer–adjust the time as needed).

- Write down the series of events on your Potty Record.

EXAMPLE 2: PUP DOES PEE OR POOP

- Put their leash on (4 to 6 foot leash rather than a retractable—allows for to much freedom and easy distraction).

- If using a bell, encourage them to ring it before going outside.

- Take your pup to their pee and poop space.

- Stand quietly and wait for them to go. (Remember, your job is to not be another distraction).

- Your Pup pees or poops.

- **Quietly** say your Pee or Poop Cue word and then 'Good boy, Good girl'. Repeat until they are finished.

- Have a party (verbally praise make it a PARTY! It's supposed to be exciting.) AND give a tasty treat.

- Write down the series of events on your Potty Record.

- Have some play time or go for a walk.

LOVE MY CRATE!

Do this little exercise in the beginning to get them to choose to go in.

- Bring your dog over to the crate but don't put them in.

- Leave the door open.

- Sprinkle the bottom of the crate with some yummy treats (use cheese, chicken, hot dogs or even beef). Leave some treats close to the entrance so your pup doesn't have to go too far to get them at first. We want to tempt them to go further in.

- Let your pup go in; don't force but encourage your pup to go into the crate.

- Let them clean up all the treats.

- Repeat this exercise until your pup is going in freely.

After multiple attempts, your pup should start to be excited about going into their crate, looking for some more treats. When this happens, move on to the steps below.

1. Sprinkle treats in the crate.

2. Close the door when your pup is eating the treats.

3. Once your pup finishes, drop some more treats in from the top (or side if you have a vari kennel) of the crate.

4. When your pup finishes and is looking to you for some more, open the door and let your pup out. They may not want to come out because of all the good stuff happening. If that's the case, reward them in the crate for staying in and then end the exercise.

5. Repeat until you are able to leave your pup in there for longer and longer periods of time with the door closed.

6. Another great way to help this process is to feed all of your pups meals in the crate. They will be running to get in before you know it.

DON'T MISS!

If you haven't read **The Secret To Getting Your Dog To Do What You Want** yet, you will want to check it out. It is available on Amazon Kindle and Audible.com.

These books are in the works and you won't want to miss them:

Turn Your Problem Pup Into Your Dream Dog

HELP! My Dog Won't Stop (Insert Behavior Here)!

Register at JennaLeeGallicchio.com to be notified of all new releases. Your dog will thank you!

URGENT PLEA!

Will You Help?

Thank you for reading Jenna's (my mom's) book! It will really help her to buy me lots of bones.

Would you kindly go back to the site where you purchased this book and leave your feedback? It helps my mom (Jenna) to make sure that she is presenting you the information in a way that is helpful to you. It will also let her know what you want so she can help you better.

If you bought this book in a store stop by her Facebook page: AllStarPaws and let her know what you thought.

ABOUT THE AUTHOR

In 2004, JennaLee Gallicchio was working in the Banking Industry as a Sales Assistant. Although not happy, she had no thought of changing careers. All that changed when she adopted a four month old puppy who would turn her world upside down. His name was Mattie.

Mattie left Jenna feeling overwhelmed, frustrated and in way over her head. It wasn't just Jenna he left feeling this way, but also her family, who all had their own dogs.

Close to deciding that the best thing would be to return him to the dog rescue where she adopted him, she decided to try one thing first. In a desperate effort, she hired a professional dog trainer, K9 Experience.

While just starting to work with Kay Anne, her dog, Sydney, died very suddenly. Extremely saddened by her loss, she also acknowledged to herself that she had no excuses and failing to make a change with Mattie was not an option.

Working with K9 Experience gave Jenna and Mattie a great start and also renewed Jenna's own personal passion for training dogs.

Completing a certification program, through Animal Behavior College, she began teaching group classes at The Barker Lounge in Roselle, NJ. She also continued to take classes with Mattie where they continued to build their relationship.

She completed Camp R.E.W.A.R.D. with Pamela Dennison and worked for a short time with Tracy Skelnar and MaryLou Hanlin, in the hopes of doing Agility. As she saw the transformation in Mattie, Jenna was inspired, even more, to learn more about the "science" behind the training. It is a road she has never looked back on.

Although Mattie is no longer with her, he left a lasting impact on her life. Because of his needs, Jenna now has the ability to teach clients how to really understand and learn from their dogs. Sharing with them and inspiring them is an extreme pleasure.

She was fortunate enough to use this training when Ryder joined her and then again with Emmy. Having a puppy is a humbling experience and it was one that was filled with laughter, and tears of frustration at times.

This is Jenna's second instructional training book. but she has many others in her head and in the works. Her first was ***The Secret To Getting Your Dog To Do What You Want.***

Thank you again to all of the wonderful readers who have taken the time to read this! It means more than you will ever know.

This book is also available in a Kindle edition or Audio form. Both can be found on Amazon.com.

ADDITIONAL BOOKS AVAILABLE:

THE SECRET TO GETTING YOUR DOG TO DO WHAT YOU WANT